poems and counterpoems
1986-1995

JUST
poems and counterpoems
1986-1995
US

Kwame Alexander

Black Words™

A Division Of The Alexander Publishing Group, Inc.

BlackWords™ Poetry Series is a Division of
The Alexander Publishing Group, Inc.
P.O. Box 21
Alexandria, VA 22313-0021

Typesetting and design by:
Zí Design, Inc.
10025 Governor Warfield Parkway, Suite 312
Columbia, Maryland 21044

Cover Design: Bill Neely & Diane Baier
Cover Artwork: John Ashford
Back Photos: Christopher Gunn

ISBN 1-888018-00-3
Library of Congress Catalogue Card Number: 95-078200

This book is composed in Letter Gothic and LucidaSans
Manufactured in the United States of America
10 9 8 7 6 5 4 3 2 1

For

The Women:	Nana, Barbara, Sia, Nataki, Fidella, Julie, Samaraca & Stacey
The Men:	Adé, E. Curtis, Percy, Sean, Eugene, Melvin & Marshall
The Children:	Nandi, Anneka, Gene Jr., Ché & Cedric
The Family:	The Alexanders, The Johnsons & The Smiths
The Nation:	All My People! *All My People!*

Acknowledgements

A special acknowledgement to my father, Dr. E. Curtis Alexander, for teaching me, over the past 27 years, the in's and out's of the publishing industry (I was listening and learning); and for the serious logo ... *So It Is Written, So It Shall Be!*

Many thanks to my family and friends who have supported me spiritually & *financially* over the years. I cannot express enough gratitude to my parents, Barbara Alexander and Dr. E. Curtis Alexander, for keeping the television turned off (except Fridays) and keeping our home filled with books (from day one). Much respect to those who came before me, particularly, my professor of three years, Nikki Giovanni and two of my greatest influences, who are also two of the *baddest* poets, Haki Madhubuti and Sonia Sanchez.

A strong *asanté sana* to the members, staff and extended family of STAGED BLACK (A Collective of Black Artists) - past and present - who have labored with me to transform the Hip Hop Arts "Movement" into a life-long commitment to Black Cultural Expression as a step towards liberation: Charlene Woelfel, Melody Burgess, Noni Dabney, Harlan Nunn, Michael Williams, Toni Blackman, Yolanda Sampson, Creativ Born True, Girard Seabrooks, E. Augustus Jones, Traysi Lenee, Malik Roots, Dave Foreman, Velator, Lori Trigg, Stephanie Stanley, Marshall Johnson, Kerri & Darryl Washington, Stephany Kelly, Chris Downing, Herb White, Marcella Usher, Greg Bargeman, Taffanie Ketema, Raquel Arrodando, John Ashford, Ray Shell, Professor Opal Moore, Catherine Smith-Jones, Jennifer Graham, The St. Louis Akimbo Crew, Angela Taylor, Rishaunda Ewing, Juanita Britton & BZB, Monda Webb, Omar Tyree, Abena Modupe, Wadud, Stephanie Renee, Gene & Kenny of Buttamilk Worldwide, Ray Llanos of Rhapsody, Esther Ivereen, Reggie Timson, David Massey, Tiffany Hamiel, D-Knowledge, Goldie, Trac Anderson, Sheila Alexis & Family, Henry & Maria Briggs, Frances Walker, Hayward Corley, Jon Palmer Claridge, Harold Sessions, Alec Bouknight and the entire Carver Community Center & Advisory Committee.

A special thanks to Tango Hill, LuWanna Glover, Raymond Wells, Joan Jackson and my colleagues and students (especially Jamila) at the Ebon International Preparatory Academy - *keep your head up* - "Education is the key."

Since my collegiate days, these two individuals have supported my ventures and extended their hearts - a warm thanks to my best friends, Marshall and Stephanie.

This book would not have been possible without the dedication and artistic professionalism of the Zí Design team, my copy editor—Katherine Cain, and my "partner," writer-extraordinaire—Stacey Evans. Lastly, a very special Asanté to Nandi & Nia for giving me five years of "experience" which makes a great portion of this book "real."

Much Love, Peace and Blessings to each of us ... *Just Us!*

Contents

The Family/The Nation

Afterword/Other Words

JUST
US

poems and counterpoems
1986-1995

Foreword/Forward

poem (pō'əm) *n.*
> an arrangement of words, esp. a rhythmical composition,
> sometimes rhymed, in a style more imaginative than ordinary
> speech.

counterpoems (Kount'ər pō'əm) *n.*
> an arrangement of words, opposed to prevailing poetic
> definitions, for the purpose of artistic and cultural effect,
> *i.e. BlackWords.*

Introduction

His poems speak of old and new. Wrapping us in words of warmth, words of controversy, words of love. Dusting off the age-old concerns of an oppressed people and presenting them in a shiny new package—complete with sound bytes, current events and personal testimony.

A masterful wordsmith, Kwame Alexander is a bad young poet. He paints pictures that can captivate the spirit and the mind. Kwame packs punch in small packages and he often economizes his words, as done in "Life:"

> *This morning*
> *I woke to find*
> *termites*
> *eating away at*
> *my home ...*
> *my friends*
> *assured me that*
> *the good*
> *liberal ones*
> *were not involved*

In dealing with the old and new, Kwame sees the beauty in Blackness, but boldly explores the ugliness. "Revolutionary Love Poem," tells us "the biggest problem facing us in the 21st century is us." His words cook up an important reminder ... love is a necessary ingredient in the recipe for revolution. Kwame's love for children is quite strong ... he touches on the issue of fatherhood in a special piece for his daughter in "That's My Daddy" and captures the spirit of brotherly love for his sister, in the poem "Sia."

Just Us is yet another extension of the African oral tradition— evidence of the continuum. The pieces here sing and dance. Buppie Blues captures the blues aesthetic in an outspoken, yet concise manner, and one can hear and feel the drums behind "Ebony Images." Each page combines text with movement and sound. One reads his poem. One hears it, feels it and cannot help but "clap your hands to what he's doing." *More bounce to the ounce of the word.*

In essence, the words between these pages inspire, enlighten and entertain. Kwame Alexander speaks to and for a new generation of artists who will definitely make the ancestors proud ... *and you too!*

Toni Blackman
Washington, DC
7/95

The Women

*The full potential of a nation
cannot be realized
unless the full potential of its women
is realized*

—Haki Madhubuti, *The Book of Life*

Our
Women

Women
Our Women
not like we own you
like you are the only women for us
it is not the faces
pale w/color we crave
we seek life
our women black/hold onto us
like sunset caressing midnight
like midnight entering sunrise
like sunrise giving birth to daylight
Sista you shine
Sista you mine
not like i own you
like i dig you
my precious black gold
and while it may be couterrevolutionary
you my diamond mine
my mind
mine - dig - you
my woman
our women
black and naturally
smooth and black
and vigorous and black
and practical and black
intellectual and black
and naturally
you fine
our women
dark-soiled earth
seeds planted in you
bring life forth
bring life force

our women black
morning mint-flavored
coffee brown black
copper shining amber
sun-burned black
ochre khaki rust
rising high yellow black
evening coal-sabled
chestnuts roasting black
late night sun-setting
pitch jet black
spadiceous
stramineous
and castaneous
our women black
and naturally
we are your men

12/94

9

Awkward
Poems

for Samaraca

Sometimes i wish we weren't friends
then i could stare deeply into your bold bright eyes
and find answers to questions i'm afraid to ask
but for now, i'll stick to quick glances ...
and other friendly gestures

Sometimes i wish we weren't friends
then i could hold your hands in ways
that made your palms moist from my wet suggestions
but for now, i'll stick to high fives ...
and other friendly gestures

Sometimes i wish we weren't friends
then i could eclipse your moon-baked
ruby-red crescents
with my sun-starved cherry-coated lips
but for now, i'll stick to light pecks ...
and other friendly gestures

Sometimes i wish we weren't friends
then i could kneel before your delicate temple
grasping you with my full arms as we lay embracing
into the morning
but for now, i'll stick to daylight hugs ...
and other friendly gestures

What i am trying to say is
I love
glancing into your big eyes
touching your soft hands
kissing your dark cheeks

hugging your warm body
... and being your friend

but one day ...
one day real soon
i'm gonna put away those
big
soft
dark
warm
friendly gestures
and get close
get real close to you

but for now, i'll stick to awkward poems ...
and other friendly gestures

10/94

Corepoem
(The Beginning)

The grasp of the earth
and the softness of the wind
were most definitely something
but not until i witnessed
the journey of a
thousand waves
through the rippling waters
of your ocean
did i understand the true
meaning of
gravity

10/89

Corepoem
(The End)

The grasp of the earth
is still
the wind
briskly breezes
past me
the once witnessed journey
of a thousand waves
has drowned
in the rippling waters of my ocean
slowly i fall
gravity no longer within reach
no longer holding
me up

4/94

Kupenda

Lips
like yours
ought to be worshiped
see i ain't never been too religious
but you can baptize me
anytime

9/94

Kupenda

With u
b/hind napping
i lay dazed
b/side
yr supple
cocoa-flavored
doe-skin

i lay dazed
w/firm thoughts
of u
my deer
running wild
and free

11/94

Note: Kupenda means "With Love" from the East African Language, Kiswahili

Kupenda

She quenched my
sun-rayed thirst
the moon-
beaming her
in/two
our life

2/90

Kupenda

Like a seed
u grew
in/to
my earth

2/95

Kupenda

Yr movement is
fluid
like a river running
deep
i am careful not to
drown

5/93

Kupenda

Wide hips
spread equally across
firm legs
sprung open
like maple syrup
poured over
whole
wheat
hotcakes

6/94

Kupenda

Silence
doesn't mean
we have run out
of things to say
only that
we are trying
not to say them

10/94

Essence

for Attorney Mary Cox, Dr. LaFrancis Rodgers-Rose, Sonia Sanchez and Susan Taylor

A deep sister
beautiful and bold and bodiful
like an ocean jumpin'
w/bumpin' waves
and thumpin' ripples
glazed in Kente
walkin' and talkin'
payin' close attention to
Everything
as her grand forehead
grooves to think beats
shinin' and glowin'
provin' that the mind is a
beautiful thing
still concentratin' on
Everything
as her teeth gleam
braids beam
lips dance
and
face smiles (a lot)
all at the same time

4/91

Sia

When mommy had you
you were mine
my sister
and sometimes
my daughter too
like the time
you wanted to swing
down on 125th
in the park
and i pushed
the little boy
out, off, and
onto the ground
so that you could
swing-
yeah, you were mine
my little baby girl
who over the course
of the years
developed into
a woman
a strong woman
a strong African woman
who can now
swing
all by herself

7/89

Mother's Day

I love you mommy
you are so special to me
Ever since that day in '68
when you brought me into this world

I could have made this poem rhyme, but
that means I would have had to really
think
When I'm with you, I shouldn't have
to think
my feelings for you are deep,
but unhidden

What can I say?
I've been with you for nearly 18 years
I've loved it and
I'm sure you have
I couldn't and wouldn't have made it
this far without you
You are the best mother in the world and
I love you

Well mommy, there is not that much else
to say
except that in me, every day is
Mother's Day.

5/86

*Note: This was my first "real" poem. My Mother still has the same frame
(I spent most of my paycheck on that frame. Back then minimum wage
was $3.35/hour) in her living room. I spent two days constructing this
poem, and just knew I was the next Langston Hughes. I publish it now,
perhaps, to show the transformation of "my words," the evolution of a
poet: 1986-1995.*

Weak
Daze

Having been immersed
in the deep study of
her culture
of poverty
she sought employMENt
during the week
to pay her delinquent
BILLs
before she was
CUT OFF from
her TELE-
vision
IT'S A BIRD
IT'S A PLANE
Noooo! it's
Friday Night
and she just got
PAID to fully
enter-vein
w/ her cosmic friends
who skate the sky
until SATURnDAY
COMES and GOES and
COMES and comes and
keeps coming
cause she's
on CALL:
waiting for
her soul
to come black
she floats into Sunday
MOURNing

and while makeshift Jesus's
are busy pREACHING
easy-go/kwik-kopy/safeway
sermons 'bout "getting to heaven"
FLYGIRL has just
come back from
her journey
above
and is now stronger and
more powerful than
never

2/93

Betty

my Betty
lives
downstairs
in 1B
looks 38 is 83
and fine
like aged wine
she steps out
of Virginia's dew
breathin' in
Newport air
on her way upstairs
to loan me bread
for my french toast
I thank her with a hug
she holds on tight like
it is her last slice
or something
when i smell the smoke
"turn that stove down, boy,
fo' you burn that bread."
And i know i better
because early mornings
wouldn't be the same
without my french toast/no
they just wouldn't be the same

5/95

Soul On Fire

for Stacey Lyn Evans

And The Sun God said "that's hip"
and it was
and she was too
i mean she was double hip
sister was so hip
when she sat down she was still standing
like some ole' Egyptian queen from way back
from way way black-
jack you diggin' it
i mean sister was
Nefertiti livin' in your neighborhood
or Sheba walkin' down your street
or if you was lucky
Cleopatra chillin' at your crib,
i mean sister was fly
so fly
and she kept getting flyer
flyer and flyer
she kept getting flyer
flyer and flyer
and i couldn't even breathe her air
on account of
my soul was on fire

And the Sun God said "that's cool"
and it was
and she was too
i mean sister was so cool
she even taught white folks how to dance
now that's her, being cool-
geographically cool, living bi*cool*stal

somewhere
between hot and cold
even her temper was lukewarm
like an infant
i was a newcomer
and she
my *cool*comer
always on time
never late-so cool
clocks stopped-
she was stopwatch cool
brothers would stop and watch
and watch and stop,
but failed to jock
thought she was too hot-
not knowing her was merely
cool-hot,
but i knew
cause i was cool too
so i bopped to her cool
on time, with my line-
say sista, you cool
and i'm cool,
so why don't we just cool out together-
but my cool was too late, cause by then
she was just
chillin'
but she was still fly,
so fly
and i
kept trying to reach her sky
climbin' higher
higher and higher

i kept climbing higher
higher and higher
and i still couldn't breathe her air
on account of
my soul was on fire

And the Sun God said "that's deep"
and it was
and she was too
i mean sister was so deep
when she looked up she saw her back-
now that's deep
even her conversations were deep
orgasmically tripping me into a black hole
of her words
like
hip
cool
and
Na kupenda Sana, baby-
can't get deeper
than she was
deep like Atlantis-
i mean you knew she was there
but you just couldn't touch her,
but i could
and i did
cause i was deep too
like a crescendo on the rise-
climbing higher
so high
so fly
so you ask me what her name was-

if you was hip to her cool
then you wouldn't have to ask
so it must be too deep for you
but i'll tell you this
she was so fly
so fly
so fly
so fly
and she kept getting flyer
flyer and flyer
and i kept climbing higher
higher and higher
and i still couldn't breathe her air,
but thank God
my soul was on fire
my soul was on fire

5/95

The Men

One thing they cannot prohibit-
the strong men ... coming on
the strong men gittin' stronger.
Strong Men ...
Stronger.

-Sterling Brown, "Strong Men"

Real Men

*for Dr. E. Curtis Alexander, Mayor Marion
Barry, Rev. Ben Chavis, and Minister Louis Farrakhan*

Why are we so scared of the men?
the real men
with vertical holds
on their backs
standing upright and tall
bowing only to their children
and the women

Why are we so scared of the men?
the real men
Black like us
w/light speed awareness
of the changing seasons in our midst
Clearing the fog w/breathtaking oratory
and backing it up w/sun-drenching actions
men who speak the truth to the people
winter spring summer and fall

Why are we so scared of the new men?
the real men
uncompromising
offensive
stern
complete and
honorable
these men carry their children
and our struggles
on their shoulders
seldom laugh (cause ain't really nothin' funny)
these men
confident in self

align themselves w/
militants, integrationists, afrocentrists, civil righters
and
other black men
in the same breath

Why are we so scared of the brave men?
the real men
able to mesh
young and aged
old and new
why are we so scared of black men
dictating new agendas for our time
why are we so scared of black men
with change in mind
why are we so scared of the men
who own the night
the real men
not dead carcasses holding up lamposts
on urban *cool*-de-sacs in Mississippi, New York.
Real black men moving beyond
the advancement of certain people
saying - meaning - doing
things that we only dream of
and think about
these things we are scared of?

it is rumored that these men
make no excuses, owe nobody
and teach us through their actions
that there is no reason
to be afraid of
Real Men

8/94

Options

On the verge of a
nervous breakdown
was a nigger mean-
ing to jump the waters
and escape the flood
of his mind and body and
who learned to smile at DaNang
would tilt his head to the wind/beat
humming the tune of a distant drummer
covered in jeans with holes sewn from
back to front
enabling his knees to see the
happenings of the neighbor's hood
wd march with Colt 45 in one hand
and Nam in the other
carrying on stimulating, exciting, breathtaking
conversation with himself
being happy and free on a
chilly December morning
shirtless bimbo lewis missed the boat
to cross his river
and on that trembling bridge
homeboy stumbled on solid rock
and tripped right into
insanity

6/88

Bullet
Proofs

for Chris Weber and Juwan Howard

1.
At game time
brothers jump for control
of their pockets
and bullets-
black and white
take off
racing for the green

2.
Ain't nothin' really wrong
bullets get shot all the time
in Landover
played out under
the hoop dreams of district teens
caught in the crossfire
of small arms aimed at large targets
for love
of money

3.
Young guns
shoot statistics
way up high
w/revolving dunks
shattering life-size goals
and bullets still lay up and down the courts
as innocent bystanders lay up and down the streets
gripping ballistics-
proving that
things still ain't changed and
you jingling brother

4.
Half-time offers new chances
at evening scores & sharpening bullets
new recruits catch breaths before taking
rehearse plays for real-life fast breaks
and buy time behind the bars
of full-time locker rooms

5.
Shots fired inside the perimeter
draw foul play
and sometimes late calls
to unsuspecting guardians
while bullets gain momentum
stealing more seconds off the clock
Tick Tock
Tick Tock

6.
Last quarter bank shots
and free throws
phatten already deep pockets
and send players back home
and send players black home
where real cagers practice
late season buzzer shots
in 5
4
3
2
1
BOOM!
and nobody ever stops to ask why
We gotta be named "The Bullets?"

1/95

Daddy

Wednesday nights don't make me feel
too good
i toss and turn
in my bed thinking of Thursday morning
the day I gotta get up extra early
to hear momma scream
"take out the trash boy"
So i get up and put on whatever
is lying on the floor next to me that
i was supposed to put in the hamper
Yesterday
then i put on my hat

Walking through the house is always fun
i can stop by the kitchen and steal
some of the cake that
momma told us not to touch
It's a good kind of feeling to be the only one up
get some milk, and watch all the fat white ladies
on TV try to lose weight
then i get some orange juice

Standing in the doorway
i see Momma with her strap-
in my mind
and quickly remember that
i'm supposed to take out all the trash
in the house
and anything else i see lying around

so then i finally get all the bags together
and take out the trash-
the more trash i find
the cleaner the house is
and the nicer she will be to us
and then i think of daddy

2/89

My Father's Eulogy

My Father
rests alone
at home
and questions
why?
His sisters
chose
another man
to pray.
The last
time
his mother
died,
they did
the same,
but he obliged
and sat beside
another man
who said goodbye
to Granny.
Only
this time
he couldn't
bear
the thought
of losing twice.
And so
at home
alone
he sat
away
from flowers
open graves

saving tears
for the future's
sure unrest
endless nights
spent reciting
his Father's Eulogy
to himself

7/95

Poet's Rite
(and they read too!)

for Marshall Johnson, Malik Roots,
Omar Tyree, Wadud & c.

We men-child
with identity unmasked-
traversing negro rivers
with typewriter in one hand
& hand grenade in the other
discovered Heritage
and Deferred Dreams
on our way *From Slavery To Freedom*

We men-child
with purpose unfeigned-
educated our thoughts to teach
Liberation Pedagogy
to *The Wretched of the Earth*
"by any means necessary"
and forced our words to mean *something*
cause some of us ain't sayin' *nothin'*

We men-child
with direction unaltered-
enlisted our egos in book camps
got stationed on *The Big Sea*
while training for cultural warfare
and armed ourselves with haversacks
complete with bulletproof journals
& stiletto ink pens
for our daily encounters with
War and sometimes *Peace*
of mind

We men-child
with identity unmasked-
coming full circle
we poets
Black first
Men second
carving out new dimensions
into first world fabric
and building new wor(l)ds
with clear messages for better tomorrows
We Black Men
undying in our quest for manhood
undaunting in our commitment to Black art
unbending in our assertion that:
We men-child
making Black poetry
out of *Dust Tracks On A*
Road Up From Slavery
To The Promised Land
cause we artists
cause we warriors
cause we understand
a Poets Rite (*and we read too!*)

6/95

The Children

Any meaningful discussion of the survival or the future of Black people must be predicated upon Black people's plan for the Maximal development of Black children.

- Dr. Frances Cress Welsing, "The Isis Papers"

Ebony
Images

Ebony ...
trapped
dark black
and lovely
brown mocha
brown black
jumpin'
double black brown
night black
outta sight black
so black
purple black
blue black
black blue
black black
blue black
black black
brown Smoked
Morrocan black
yellow black
mellow yellow
black brown
positive chocolate
brown black
Free
Black
... Images

8/87

Nature
vs.
Nurture

The six-year-old asked her mommy
"when can I get a doll?"
the mommy replied,
"Not until Christmas, dear!"

The 12 year-old asked his father
"Can I get a baseball mit, all the boys have them?"
the father answered
"Maybe on your birthday"

The 36-year-old father
asked his four year-old daughter
"Would you like a treat"
she responded
"No, I'll wait for Halloween"

3/90

Ade'
(My definition
of friendship)

Spittin'
watermelon seeds
from my sticky-smooth
fried chicken lips
and slurpin
icy-25 cent
melted freezy cups
on the stoop
with
Craig
everyday

11/89

44

That's My Daddy

for Nandi Assata Alexander

That's my daddy
she says
at the park
to troy and dana
when they ask
"can you push us too"
in the swing

That's my daddy
she says
at her school
to kierra and daniel
when they plead
"can we sit down too"
on your lap

That's my Nandi
i say
in my soul
to myself
when they ask
"who's that, over there"
and she says
"That's My Daddy."

5/95

Southern Africa
(A New Vision)

And when the children ask
about Africa's past
we will tell them the liberating truth
about our oppression
about our repression
about our impressions of Southern Africa
but when they want to know about tomorrow
we will not leave their futures grim and hollow

And when the children ask
about apartheid's lash
we won't hide the facts
that broke the backs
of African Blacks
who carried the sacks
of diamonds
of diamonds
but when they want to know about tommorrow
we will not fill their souls with pain and sorrow

And when the children ask
why are we dying so fast
in Southern Africa?
we will tell them of the famine
we will tell them of the drought
we will tell them of the sick diseases
and what these vicious wars are about
and when they want to know about tomorrow
and when they want to know about tomorrow
we will tell them of yesterday
but also of today
about the other side
that the media hides

about Malawi
it's political stride
about Mozambeecan refugees
returning home
yes we will tell them what today has shown
about Tanzania, Angola, and Namibia
Botswana, Lesotho, and Zamibia
and when all is said and done
Yes they will know of Biko and Sisulu
that Mandela was imprisoned
but they will also know of Southern Africa
and it's new vision
to be free of famine
to be free of disease
to be free of neo-colonialism
to be free of corruption
to be free
to be free
to be free
in Southern Africa

9/94

NOTE: This poem was composed for the Southern African Educational
Campaign in Washington, D.C.

Nandi's Prayer

for our children

Creator
Asanté for another day
Asanté for a chance to play

Tafadali, watch over me
watch over my mommy
watch over my daddy and
the rest of my family

Now, I'll sleep to rest my soul
When I wake, I'll again be whole

Na Kupenda Sana

Amen

12/93

Note: Written for my daughter Nandi during Kwanzaa 1993. In the East African Language of Ki-swahili, Asanté means "Thank You;" Tafadali means "Please;" Na Kupenda Sana means "I Love You." Please feel free to share it with your children.

The Family/The Nation

*A people losing sight of origins are dead. A
people deaf to purposes are lost ... The eyes of
seers should range far into purposes. The ears of
hearers should listen far towards origins.*
        -Ayi Kwei Armah, "Two Thousand Seasons"

*Got up this morning
feeling good and Black
thinking Black thoughts
did Black things
played all my Black records
and minded my own Black bidness*

*Put on my best Black clothes
walked out my Black door
and ...
Lord Have Mercy
White
Snow!*
        -Jackie Earley, "1,968 Winters"

Revolutionary
Love Poem

I once read a lovepoem at a revolutionary meeting

You with your nubian glare
that lights up
my world
our world
THE WORLD
(a blessing in the skies)
I feel yr presence perfect
like a single rain/drop
S
P
L
A
S
H
I
N
G

S P L A T T E R I N G
from my head
down to my toes
smile and you show me the moonbeam
quenching my soulful thirst
w/starburst flavor
I melt (in yr arms)

and nobody clapped.
I once read a lovepoem at a revolutionary meeting

The Sun melted slowly
the day you left

and when you called
I froze

and the brothers shouted,
"ain't that counterrevolutionary, talk about the man!"

I once read a lovepoem at a revolutionary meeting

On lonely nights
while second-floor
traffic noises
loom through the air
I dream of being in
yr blackride ...
sometimes driving

and the sisters screamed
"ain't gone' be no cars in the revolution,
talk about the man"

I once read a lovepoem at a revolutionary meeting

I am a dawn ocean
thrusting my midnight waves
onto yr sandy shore
until yr tide comes ...
in

and they told me to
"Sit down,"
cause I won't talking about the revolution

The next time I read a lovepoem at a revolutionary meeting,
I'll make sure and tell the "revolutionaries" that
there will be no revolution
until we learn how to respect our women
until we learn how to treat our men
until we learn how to love each other
I'll make sure I tell the "revolutionaries" that
fightin' "the man" is moot if we ain't got a plan
to start lovin' one another
I'll make sure I tell the revolutionaries that
the biggest problem facing us in the 21st century is
us

once we love
we can create
You Dig?
Well if not,
then dig yourself a black hole and peep this ...

They asked me to read a blacklovepoem
at a revolutionary meeting

Got up this morning
feeling good and black
hugged my Black wife
kissed my Black child
ate Black food
took my daughter to a Black school
and shopped at all Black stores

Came back to my Black house
opened my Black mind
and ...
Lord Have Mercy
A
Revolution!

2/94

Life

for Professor Derrick Bell

This morning
I woke to find
termites
eating away at
my home...
my friends
assured me that
the good
liberal ones
were not involved

2/93

54

Freedum
(A WakeUp Call)

Yesterday
they wouldn't let us go to their schools
wouldn't let us read
wouldn't let us write
made us work in the fields
and never get paid to toil
for them
And today
they let us go to their schools
teach us to read
teach us to write
let us work in any field
and always get paid to toil
for them

And we talkin' 'bout tomorrow
better be better than yesterday
cause today we got 11 year-old nintendo-totin'
roughnecks raping our daughters
cause today we got seven year-old barbie-collectin'
homegirls getting raped by our sons
no sense
no sense
no sense
no censorship?

The *Boys in the Hood* are getting much too *Fresh*
w/the gangsta b's from *New Jack City* so they run
Straight Outta Brooklyn heading for *South Central*
looking for *Juice* so they can become
Menaces to Society or better yet
Natural Born Killers or
Natural Born Killers or
Natural Born Killers

And we talkin' bout a better tomorrow
better be better than today
see yesterday we had better
better teachers
better schools
better parents *well they were*
cause back in the day
every woman seemed *six feet high*
and when yo mama wasn't around
like she was at work
they was
and when yo daddy wasn't around
like he was workin'
they was
and today if you say hello to the wrong little
somebody's ten-year-old
you end up *six feet deep*
cause u living in a world where
Barney is making more money
than the President
Rodney Allen Rippy is living up on 127th and Lenox
w/Fat Albert
waiting for a shout out from Bart Simpson
the 21st Century's answer to
What Time Is It Black People?
Snoop doggy dogg is the next Stokely Carmichael
the Black Panthers have evolved into doggy doggs
and the only piece of information
kids remember about the 60's is
H. Rap Brown's middle name and
whatever happened to Shakur
2Pac that is

And we talkin' 'bout tomorrow
teach the children the truth today
teach the children the truth today
put one and one together
put two and two together
put three black men in a history textbook
and what do you get?
Martin Luther King
Martin Luther King
Martin Luther King
see yesterday we had dreams of
better tomorrows and brighter futures
but today we still dreamin' bout
better tomorrows and brighter futures
still dreamin'
'bout reparations
ancient Black nations
freeing up Haitians
post-integration
equal education
and birthday celebrations
I Have A Dream
I Have A Dream
I Have A Dream
and in that dream
I wish that Black people
would start learning from yesterday
stop dreaming about tomorrow
and wake up
Today!

9/94

Conflicting
Interest

for Pamela

The struggle for
Black liberation
must be prepared for different
ideologies and different
solutions
so u and i can
disagree, discuss, and any other
dissing we want to do
as long as we realize
that what u and i think
is not as important as
The Struggle for
Black Liberation

9/89

Manpower

Appetizer:
Strawberries, orange slices,
pineapples, grapes, apples.
So I ask her,
"What about the Watermelon?"
She reads me like a page out of the
Afrolistic Guide to Nutrition:
You never mix citrus fruits with melons.

Start with the scratch and there will be no itch
we must return to the old ways
to the old way
abandon that which is new and confusing
just because it's modern, don't make it real
it just be-come-temporary
like my job.

Paid $536 a week to smile at corporate-fearing
would be tarzans, with jungled bellies who make
$536/day to smile at corporate-wannabe's who
waste no time making well-thought of jokes about
O.J.

Obey Your Thirst. Drink Sprite. Obey Your Drink.
Thirst Sprite. Drink Your Sprite. Obey Thirst.
Thirst Your Drink. Obey Sprite. Obey Sprite.
Obey Sprite?

The Blacker the smile, the sweeter the pension.
The slower the walk, the faster the lynching.

We remember ROOTS, the latest version,
written, directed, produced, created, marketed, and
starring ...

Introduction: I don't recall
pt 1: The untouchable airborne nigger
pt 2: The innocent crotch-grabbing
"more than black" nigger
and the saga continues with:
pt 3: The most recent unstoppable airport nigger.

Caution niggers: *Mixing citrus fruits with melons is
hazardous to you and your health.*

Lately everything has become sexual
the way you walk
the way we talk
and even my job has become sexual:
Want to stick my disk in the drive
and load my software
ERROR! unable to read disk
the program worked last week
so i checks my hardware
and discover that the problem is my memory
I discover that the problem is my memory.

Was it French or Italian. The tomatoes and olives
should be seasoned with feta cheese. Break the
lettuce into 1/2 inch pieces and then add the crou-
tons and radishes. Mix everything in one bowl
and chill.

We walk the slow walk
the walk of zombies in snow
we don't owe nobody
don't own nobody
and don't know nobody who listens to
Garth Brooks
Khallid Muhammad maybe
but not Garth Brooks
Leonard Jeffries maybe
but not Garth Brooks
Maulana Karenga maybe
but not Garth Brooks
Professor Egypt himself
but not Garth Brooks
How you gonna practice an ancient philosophy
in 1994
and expect it to work for you when it didn't work for
them in 4
Silly rabbits, *Afrosintricks* are for kids
grown-ups walk in the sun
avoid snow at all costs
and attend narrow nationalist pre-Afro historic
lectures
as much as they listen to
Garth Brooks.

The phone rings
it's 6:30
it's not her.

Fresh green peppers, diced onions,
marinated in tamari overnight
mushrooms sauteed in olive oil for three minutes.

I remove the package of Japanese stir-fry vegetables
from the freezer
where they have been sitting overnight.

Enter mock duck
not real duck
fake duck
fake deal
Real Late!

She's supposed to be here
I'm supposed to be finished
supposin' it's 8:00 and she still ain't here
supposin' the game is on in one hour
supposin' she comes at 8:45 and expects to eat
supposin' she don't call
she don't
supposin' i sit down to eat by myself
supposin' i finish eating and sit down to watch
the game
supposin' i find that the game has been pre-empted
by another game:
I thought he retired
Maybe him just tired.

Replenish the body Black people
feed the mind African people
Reawaken the soul Sun people
Chakula for the children
Food for the dissatisfied buppies
Chakula for the CBC
Food for the NAACP

BET
BDP
BBD?
u and me
everything that survives on this planet needs food.

ask the questions poets
answer the questions scientists
probe the mind
teach the truth
grow the child
till the soil
plant the earth
work the body
study the mind
watch the people
love the people
love the people
love the people
cross the desert of your black mind
cross the desert of your mind
sprinkle water on black brain cells
sprinkle water on your brain cells
reward your desert with spring water

Return to the way
of the flow
of the water
of our people

Beware: the wrong river will take you to distant
places, like Wacko, Texas, and South Carolina high-
ways, and 7 X 9 foot cells, and separated marriages,

and lonely nights and tapped phones, and
repossessed cars, and ripped condoms, and overdue
flowers, and 9-5's, and renovated plantations, and
late-retirements, and multiple-organ failures, and
late dates, and late dates, and *late dates.*

Glancing at the paystub
on the kitchen table-
i wonder
when will i get tired of this job
the three month itch is almost up
when will i retire, or better yet
when will they tire of me

I mix the citrus fruits with the melons
the Knicks with the Rockets
and escape to the TV room where
i eat three months of
insecurity
pain
laughter and
joy in three minutes
I, stood up, contemplate
whether leaving
the juice
would make me any less *afronihilistic*
suddenly, the phone rings
at 10:30 pm
i answer
the voice asks
"how are you"
it's her:

She,
who doesn't see the wine
and the glasses
and the vegetables
and the duck
and the juice
and the juice
and my tears

"Didn't i tell you i had to get my hair done today"
hair today, gone tomorrow
she asks what's on my mind
i hesitate, wondering whether i should tell her that
i mixed the citrus fruits with the melons
instead i choose to calm her unnecessary guilt-
ridden simplicity with the fruitful culmination of my
evening-long introspection:
Everybody's Conscious, but When We Gonna Eat!

7/94

Dialogue
with Destiny

Out of
brother talk
sister talk
THE STRUGGLE
about the plight
of the people
plannin' a war
in the kitchen
brother to a sister:
"negros, negros, negros"
she agreein'
about the plight
and the talk
the nation-buildin'
the new Afrikan nation
in the bedroom
black nationalistic
input
pan-afrikanistic
output
spiritual union
comes ...

7/89

Manpower II

I own the day
and the night
I whisper at dinner
"when I'm with you"
I think ... I feel ... I be

I Be ... Ib ... IBM
owns the day from 9-5
honing the mediocre talents
of incompetent aged-yuppies
who pace dim-lit hallways on sunny days
asking pertinent questions
like "What time you leaving today"
alongside their self-proclaimed "Afro-Asian from
India-West Afrika-Tekkie, been changed-I'm American
Subordinates"
who configure systems
and upgrade memory
but seem to forget that back home, off-shore,
people seldom leave and
ain't nobody on-line

Let the circle be un-broken black people
round the edges of our squared realities
it don't matter if Mike is back
McBacon Deluxes, Boxing gloves, basketball shoes
Youth summits, new albums, new faiths, new wives,
and new evidence
and ain't gone hide the fact
that OJ is black
that OJ is black.

Image is everything. Everything is image. Is image
everything? Everything image is everything Image.
Is everything image? Imagine …

Imagine
she whispers back
with careful phrasing
"if at day, the sun refused to shine
and at night the stars didn't come out to play
who would bring the light?
who would bring delight?"

I smile hoping my bright
intentions will answer her question
correctly. And they do, somewhere
between day and night we
retreat under evening covers
probing each other with conversations
about children's names, "bad boys,"
poetry circles, and how hard it is to
cook chicken thighs all the way through
especially when you a vegetarian

When I'm with you
I own the night
even if my days have become
endless periods of encapsulated stress
highlighted by tired negros with no purpose
other than to act like they real
even if my days have become
heated debates with one-sided colleagues
who don't even know *that they don't even know*

even if my days have become
property of IBM and Bell Atlantic
and Citibank and MBNA and "Made in the USA"
is what the sister from Senegal replied
when i asked her
about the origins of her mud-dye bag
she said it was cheaper.

the darker the skin, the brighter the shine
the further the soul, the whiter the mind

Wake up Black people
open your eyes
Wake up Black people.
shuck the jive
Wake up Black People
check the ego
Wake Up Black People
learn to grow
Wake up Black people
test the truth
test the truth
Wake Up!

This morning I dreamt
I woke with you
again hungry
for hope & peace
but both were spoiled with reality doses
of corporate alarm clocks, classified waste,
uncooked thighs, good ideas, $500 phone bills,

Nandi's kindergarten blues, gun-totin' nephews,
exploded head-starts, New Jersey Drives and
pale squares and cyclic black lives and cyclic black
lives and cyclic black lives

I own the day
and the night
I whisper at breakfast
"when I'm with you"
I feel ... I think ... I be. I be Fine

Kwame 4/95

Mind Models
(We Think Of You)

for Haki Madhubuti

When deeds replace words
when actions speak loud as drizzling rains
on tinted panes
we think of you
the springwater in our desert
the sandy shores of our sea
you quench our thirstful ambitions and we wash
we watch yr back

Blacklife we treasure
you protect
where you flow there is supposed to be
no regeneration
and still you keep movin in impossible directions
guiding hungry black minds (and bellies)
to food (for thought)
and we recognize your efforts/and we think of you

It is said consciousness begins at home,
but sometimes
when one leaves home, one loses consciousness
but not you, cause you cool
like that
and more than cool
cause it ain't always about being cool
See Black America is burning up
the fires in the mirror beam reflections of
Crown Heights
Bensonhurst
Howard Beach
Southeast

South Central
and the other day
I asked a group of young Black men
what made them special
what made them unique
what made them
and one little brother smiled and replied
"I live in Southside"
and I thought of you
offering reachable hopes and new visions
affordable destinations and clear paths
I thought of you
the bold and sharp-eyed amongst us
the ressurrected, honest in search amongst us
the responsible, urgent in voice amongst us
I thought of you/we think of you
who clearly determined for us that
role models went out
when drive-by's and AIDS came in
and while the world may be a stage
the only roles for us are
doers
seers
and movers

When significant deeds replace revolutionary rhetoric
when meaningful actions speak loud as
earthquakes & winter storms
when role models willfully evolve/transform/become
mind models
We think of you
We think of you
We think of you
We think of you
and say thanks!

72
1/95

Our
Celebration

In the midst of all the
holly-jolly-mistletoe-Xmas perpetration
We Black People step in and
catch the falling star
Kwanzaa!
            Do you hear me?
KWANZAA,
the voice of millions,
some alive, others living in us

And so we remember the seeds
of our blossomed souls
We Black people jump in and
change the
"i'ma buy her everything she wants" attitude
cause our skin is gettting hip
to the coldness of January-
the month of past-due bills
and 75% off everything
We scream KWANZAA?
            Are you diggin' it?
Dig it! cause if you don't, they will
and guess who falls?

Kwanzaa
A Black hole full of Umoja
A Black hole full of Kujichagulia
A Black Hole Full of Ujima
A Black Hole Full of Ujamaa
A Black Hole full of Nia
A Black Hole of Kuumba
A Black Hole full of Imani

a full of life
I say Kwanzaa
I say Kwanzaa
The celebration of millions,
some alive,
others living
in us

12/92

Afterword/Other Words

*This Generation of Black Writer/Poets inherits
the legacy of words wielded as weapons by our
aesthetic predecessors: Baraka, Sanchez, The
Last Poets, and the age-old "Black and Unknown
Bards" that James Weldon Johnson spoke of. We
inherit a legacy of struggle, because the world is
not the beautiful place that our ancestors wrote,
sang, marched, lived and ultimately died to
bring onto existence ... Black poetry, in this era,
continues to expand the dimensions of the way in
which we think of ourselves and fuse the
"unreconciled strivings" DuBois spoke of as the
Double Consciousness ... Write On*

- Jelani Cobb

The Black
Poets

for Gwendolyn Brooks

Blk Poets
r like
dk cavities
filled w/sharp
metal/mental
images
surrounded by
crisp whiteness

In other words
we bad
Yeah, We Be Real Baad!

9/94

Buppie
Blues

I'm not Black
I'm too light
don't call me African
I want to be White

Sure, I've heard of Africa
but it's not my homeland
it belongs to all those niggers
and that man, Tarzan

I come from a place
that is color-blind
didn't eat no chicken
just steak and wine

So y'all stop fussing
and fighting for rights
just sit back like me
and act like whites

7/89

It's A Black Thing
(The Problem)

It all started on a beach called Croatan
And now it's known all over the land
They came from near and far just to have a little fun
and enjoy themselves under the September sun

But as the years went by, many problems arose
as the local residents began to turn up their nose
So they got with the city to devise a plan
of how to keep black feet off their snow white sand

So the party was then shifted up to the main strip
And the people of Virginia Beach really started to trip!!!
I've never seen so many cops just hanging around, but
if my house was being robbed, they couldn't be found
Just harrassing the masses for no reason at all.
With their crooked little grins, Oh, they were having a ball

They called us law-breaking vandals, who were out on
the take
but where were their kids "funnin" on their Spring Break?
Tell me the difference as you check the situation...
It's not the location, it's the pigmentation

It's my skin, my friends-don't let them tell you it's not
They're just trying to take away the dignity I've got

This ain't Montgomery or Selma of 1963
Ain't no brothers or sisters of mine gonna hang on
no tree
We've got to stop the madness... at the drop of a
dime ... because it's the time ... in 89 ... the bottom
line ... you know the time ... It's a black thing

YOU NOW UNDERSTAND

9/89

*Note: This poem was written by an anonymous student after the 1989
Greekfest Incident where Virginia Beach Residents, Business Owners,
Police Squads and National Guardsmen harrassed Black College Students
for four days, much in the same way civil righters were harrassed
during the 1960's. This event was a foreshadowing to the treatment
Black students received at Freaknic, held in Atlanta, Georgia. Croatan is
a small beach on the outskirts of Virginia Beach, often visited by well-to-
do whites.*

It's A Black Thing
(A Solution)

"It's A Black Thing ... You Now Understand"
the next step now is to devise a plan
cause they beat our butts at Greekfest 89
and if we go back next year, they will have whipped our
minds

"Fight the Power" is what we scream
but, sometimes I think Pay the Power is what we mean
ain't no sense in "funnin'" on their snow white land
when we can party and trip on our own black land

Think about the ramifications
of moving Greekfest to a new location
"we won't support businesses, as you'll soon discover ...
there's a place for us waiting, and it's owned by a brother"

If we're really down and want to "do for self"
then let's unify and collect our wealth
because the time is now, this second, this hour
"we gonna stop the madness," by building us some
power

Sisters and Brothers, "We Can Make It Together"
Going down to the James River would really be clever

The time is now ... Control your purse string ...
Let's do the right thing ... Cause in '90 we'll sing ...
We got our own thing ... It's a Black thing!!!

YOU BETTER UNDERSTAND

9/89

Note: This poem was written as a response to the previous poem, and was circulated around various colleges and universities, to make students aware of a new festival that would replace Greekfest. "AfreeFest" was scheduled to be held in September of 1990 on a Large Plot of land on the James River, owned by Judge Joseph Jordan (1927-1991).

Getting Away
With Murder

Upon
receiving
a final grade of
"A *minus*"
in a
Black
Women's
Studies
course
taught by an
educated
white
woman
intellectual
I Loaded

7/89

Tuesday,
December 13th, 1994

for the brothers & sisters of It's Your Mug Poetry Cafe in
Washington, D.C.

In the beginning
we spoke as liberators
freeing up space in Black brains
offering new directions for Black minds
spreading much love to Black hearts

In the beginning
we spoke the truth to the people
not even knowing completely
what it was
what it is
what it's gon' be
spoke the truth
cause we felt good inside
inspired inside
rocked inside
The Mug
and u felt good too
intellectually
emotionally
physically
not just comically
unlike today
unmoved
unattached
unless
we laughing

In the beginning
we spoke the word

conceptualizing
analyzing
and dramatizing
the word
now we poets with poet formulas
for appreciation
acceptance
and applause
dig it
6 catchy phrases
5 niggas
4 cliches
3 orgasms
2 bitches
and *one 'ho*
don't constitute no poem

In the beginning
we fused thought with
imagination
lit profound candles
and played mind games with Websters
using foreign dialect
to spin metaphors 'round
some 'ole Ebony Images
and you still laughed
and you still laughed
and it was ok
and it still is

'Cause in the beginning
even Langston was funny
making us
laugh
and think
and feel
to keep from crying
but today
things have changed
and in the end
if we don't
our poetic licenses
will be revoked
and the only liberating voices
on Tuesday nights
will be the late-night drive-by's
heard
outside
The Mug

12/94

Amerikkka

Trapped in a beautifully
deceiving white house
where every turn
is yet another wall
of colored paleness
or paled color

Built those walls with
battered hands and tortured souls
darker than the empty walls
hallowed by the false
intentions of honest men

It was '63
when my hopes were your games
my game has now started
if you dare play
but beware:
the virtue of patience no longer
lives here
for it has been sold for:
40 acres and a mule
Anger speaks while
drizzling rains crawl down
from blackened skies
as your prejudiced white house
dances to the securities of
your God

But behold, alas
My God has showered
a loud rain of perfect storms
that tear down pale walls
and move empty white houses
to make room for
our homes

7/89

Apartheid?

Imagine ...
One armed man
in your home
tie you up
call you nigger
kill your father *shoot the captain*
rape your sister *break the bunks*
burn your brother *feed the sharks*
kill your mother *sink the ship*
Call you NIGGER
why not kill you?
no need,
killed your spirit
there,
Understand?

4/88

Kwanzaa Is, Kwanzaa Ain't

Kwanzaa is
Kwanzaa ain't
Kwanzaa is
Kwanzaa ain't
Kwanzaa is...Umoja/Unity
little brothers and sisters laughing, talking, playing,
walking, working & thinking
thinking 'bout things other than barney and bart
thinking 'bout themselves - together
kwanzaa ain't
little brothers and sisters sitting around dead trees
stargazing, waiting for some overweight lie
to come gliding, sliding
down some chimney

Kwanzaa is
Kwanzaa ain't
Kwanzaa is
Kwanzaa ain't
Kwanzaa is...Kujichagulia/Self-determination
young black artists making their art-work, pay, live
sometimes leaving their $20/hour jobs with the
IBM's of the world
for poetic happiness
Kwanzaa ain't
young black men and women unhappily
rushing to their 9-5's
rushing to their cramped cubicles
rushing to their assistant to the assistant to the
assistant positions
unhappily rushing rushing rushing hurriedly
unhappily rushing to their
deaths

Kwanzaa is
Kwanzaa ain't
Kwanzaa is
Kwanzaa ain't
Kwanzaa is Ujima/Collective Work and Responsibility
is politicians rising from the abyss of spiritual chaos
to the realms of rejuvenation, rebirth and
reawakening ...
is community members lifting those weak amongst
us to positions of strength together
... is Marion Barry
Kwanzaa ain't irresponsible (move) politicians (move)
consistently (move) engaged in self-destructive
(move) behaviors (move) ain't Wilson Goode

Kwanzaa is
Kwanzaa ain't
Kwanzaa is
Kwanzaa ain't
Kwanzaa is Ujamaa
Cooperative Economics
ain't Malcolm T-shirts made in Korea
is Nia
Purpose
ain't colored overweight lies sliding down chimneys
is Kuumba
Creativity
ain't 35mm gangster templates for new jack films
is Imani
Faith
Is Imani
Faith

The next time someone asks you
What is Kwanzaa?
Tell them
Kwanzaa is
Kwanzaa ain't
Kwanzaa is
Kwanzaa ain't
Kwanzaa is
Kwanzaa

12/94

Just Us

Black poems will
feed Black Minds but
who will put chakula
into the children's bellies
and make them full with nourishment

Black poems will
cleanse Black souls but
who will give proper attention
to sisters hungry for time
and respect

Black poems will
love thin sheets of white paper but
who will develop proud black youth
who will nurture thick black hearts
who will create strong black families

It must be us ...
Just Us!

8/94

About the Author

Kwame Alexander has edited three anthologies of Black poetry: *Survival in Motion, Wake Up* and *The Flow*. He has read and performed poetry at colleges and universities throughout the country including Duke University, Temple University, Howard University and Fisk University. As a performance poet, he has toured nightclubs and concert halls across the United States and in Europe. He is the founder and artistic director of STAGED BLACK, a performing arts company based in Arlington, Virginia. A winner at the 4th National Black Arts Festival Poetry Slam Competition in Atlanta, Georgia, Kwame is currently working on a poetry/jazz/hip hop project and a second collection of poems, entitled *Kupenda*. Alexander is editor of the BlackWords Poetry Series and President of The Alexander Publishing Group. A graduate of Virginia Tech, he is the proud father of Nandi Assata Alexander.

About BlackWords™

BlackWords™ is a ground-breaking poetry series designed to produce, publish, and promote a literature that represents the ideas and ideals of a new generation of Black poets. Our line of high-quality books are created to make sure you experience true "edu-tainment," whether it be through romantic sonnets, revolutionary notes or just plain poetic vibes. BlackWords™ is all that ... *Written words that open the minds and speak to the Souls of Black Folk*.

For readings, performances, publishing opportunities and other information, please call The Alexander Publishing Group, Inc. at 1-800-614-1373.